David Bowie

By

I0435471

Michael C. Enwerem

Table of Contents

Preface

David Robert Jones (8 January 1947 – 10 January 2016), known as David Bowie was an English singer, songwriter, multi-instrumentalist, record producer, arranger, painter and actor.

He was a figure in popular music for over five decades, and was considered by critics and other musicians as an innovator, particularly for his work in the 1970s. Bowie stopped concert touring after 2004, and last performed live at a charity event in 2006. In 2013, he returned from a decade-long recording hiatus, remaining musically active until his death from liver cancer three years later.

Bowie developed an interest in music while at school where he excelled at playing the recorder. When he left school he studied art, music and design, and became fluent on the saxophone, forming his first band, that year, at the age of 15. He embarked on a professional career as a musician in 1963, and received his first management contract shortly afterwards. "Space Oddity" became his first top five entry on the UK Singles Chart after its release in July 1969. After a three-year period of experimentation, he re-emerged in 1972 during the glam rock era with his flamboyant and androgynous alter ego Ziggy Stardust. The character was spearheaded by his single "Starman" and album The Rise and Fall of Ziggy Stardust and the Spiders from Mars. The relatively short-lived Ziggy persona proved to be one facet of a career marked by reinvention, musical innovation and visual presentation.

In 1975, Bowie achieved his first major American crossover success with the number-one single "Fame" and the album Young Americans, which the singer characterized as "plastic soul". The sound constituted a radical shift in style that initially alienated many of his UK devotees. He then confounded the expectations of both his record label and his American audiences by recording the electronic-inflected album Low (1977), the first of three collaborations with Brian Eno later known as the "Berlin Trilogy". Followed with "Heroes" (1977) and Lodger (1979), each album reached the UK top five and received lasting critical praise. After uneven commercial success in the late 1970s, Bowie had UK number ones with the 1980 single "Ashes to Ashes", its parent album Scary Monsters (And Super Creeps), and "Under Pressure". He then reached a new commercial peak in 1983 with Let's Dance, which yielded several successful singles. Throughout the 1990s and 2000s, Bowie continued to experiment with musical styles, including industrial and jungle. Bowie also had a successful but sporadic film career. His acting roles include the eponymous character in The Man Who Fell to Earth (1976), Major Celliers in Merry Christmas, Mr. Lawrence (1983), the Goblin King Jareth in Labyrinth (1986), Pontius Pilate in The Last Temptation of Christ (1988), and Nikola Tesla in The Prestige (2006), among other film and television appearances and cameos.

Bowie's impact, as described by biographer David Buckley, "*challenged the core belief of the rock music of its day*." Music reviewer Brad Filicky wrote that over five decades, Bowie was "*a musical chameleon, changing and dictating trends as much as he has altered his style to fit, influencing fashion and pop culture.*" Throughout his career, he sold an estimated 140 million records worldwide. In the UK, he was awarded nine Platinum album certifications, eleven Gold and eight Silver, and in the US, received five Platinum and seven Gold certifications. He was inducted into the Rock and Roll Hall of Fame in 1996.

Chapter 1

A Brief Introduction to the early Life of Bowie

Bowie was born in Brixton, south London. His mother, Margaret Mary "Peggy" (nee Burns), from Kent, worked as a waitress, while his father, Haywood Stenton "John" Jones, from Yorkshire, was a promotions officer for the children's charity Barnardo's. The family lived at 40 Stansfield Road, near the border of the south London areas of Brixton and Stockwell. Bowie attended Stockwell Infants School until he was six years old, acquiring a reputation as a gifted and single-minded child and a defiant brawler.

In 1953 Bowie moved with his family to the suburb of Bromley, where, two years later, he progressed to Burnt Ash Junior School. His voice was considered "adequate" by the school choir, and he demonstrated above-average abilities in playing the recorder. At the age of nine, his dancing during the newly introduced music and movement classes was strikingly imaginative: teachers called his interpretations "vividly artistic" and his poise "astonishing" for a child. The same year, his interest in music was further stimulated when his father brought home a collection of American 45s by artists including Frankie Lymon and the Teenagers, the Platters, Fats Domino, Elvis Presley and Little Richard. Upon listening to "Tutti Frutti", Bowie would later say, "*I had heard God*". Presley's impact on him was likewise emphatic according to him, "*I saw a cousin of mine dance to ... 'Hound Dog' and I had never seen her get up and be moved so much by anything. It really impressed me, the power of the music. I started getting records immediately after that*." By the end of the following year he had taken up the ukulele and tea-chest bass and begun to participate in skiffle sessions with friends, and had started to play the piano.

After taking his eleven plus exam at the conclusion of his Burnt Ash Junior education, Bowie went to Bromley Technical High School.

Bowie studied art, music and design, including layout and typesetting. After Terry Burns, his half-brother, introduced him to modern jazz, his enthusiasm for players like Charles Mingus and John Coltrane led his mother to give him a plastic alto saxophone in 1961; he was soon receiving lessons from a local musician. Bowie received a serious injury at school in 1962 when his friend George Underwood punched him in the left eye during a fight over a girl. Doctors feared he would become blind in that eye. After a series of operations during a four-month hospitalization, his doctors determined that the damage could not be fully repaired and Bowie was left with faulty depth perception and a permanently dilated pupil. Despite their altercation, Underwood and Bowie remained good friends, and Underwood went on to create the artwork for Bowie's early albums.

Graduating from his plastic saxophone to a real instrument in 1962, Bowie formed his first band at the age of 15. Playing guitar-based rock and roll at local youth gatherings and weddings, the Konrads had a varying line-up of between four and eight members, Underwood among them. When Bowie left the technical school the following year, he informed his parents of his intention to become a pop star. His mother promptly arranged his employment as an electrician's mate. Frustrated by his band-mates' limited aspirations, Bowie left the Konrads and joined another band, the King Bees. He wrote to the newly successful washing-machine entrepreneur John Bloom inviting him to "*do for us what Brian Epstein has done for the Beatles—and make another million.*" Bloom did not respond to the offer, but his referral to Dick James's partner Leslie Conn led to Bowie's first personal management contract.

Conn quickly began to promote Bowie. The singer's debut single, "Liza Jane", credited to Davie Jones and the King Bees, had no commercial success. Dissatisfied with the King Bees and their repertoire of Howlin' Wolf and Willie Dixon blues numbers, Bowie quit the band less than a month later to join the Manish Boys, another blues outfit, who incorporated folk and soul—"*I used to dream of being their Mick Jagger*", Bowie was to recall. "I Pity the Fool" was no more successful than "Liza Jane", and Bowie soon moved on again to join the Lower Third, a blues trio strongly influenced by the Who. "You've Got a Habit of Leaving" fared no better, signalling the end of Conn's contract. Declaring that he would exit the pop world "to study mime at Sadler's Wells", Bowie nevertheless remained with the Lower Third. His new manager, Ralph Horton, later instrumental in his transition to solo artist, soon witnessed Bowie's move to yet another group, the Buzz, yielding the singer's fifth unsuccessful single release, "*Do Anything You Say*".

Dissatisfied with his stage name as Davy (and Davie) Jones, which in the mid-1960s invited confusion with Davy Jones of the Monkees, Bowie renamed himself after the 19th-century American frontiersman Jim Bowie and the knife he had popularized. His April 1967 solo single, "The Laughing Gnome", using speeded-up thus high-pitched vocals, failed to chart. Released six weeks later, his album debut, David Bowie, an amalgam of pop, psychedelia, and music hall, met the same fate. It was his last release for two years.

Bowie met dancer Lindsay Kemp in 1967 and enrolled in his dance class at the London Dance Centre. He commented in 1972 that meeting Kemp was when his interest in image "*really blossomed*". "*He lived on his emotions, he was a wonderful influence. His day-to-day life was the most theatrical thing I had ever seen, ever. It was everything I thought Bohemia probably was. I joined the circus*. He said"

Studying the dramatic arts under Kemp, from avant-garde theatre and mime to commedia Bowie became immersed in the creation of personae to present to the world. Satirizing life in a British prison, meanwhile, the Bowie-penned "*Over the Wall We Go*" became a 1967 single for Oscar; another Bowie composition, "*Silly Boy Blue*", was released by Billy Fury the following year. In January 1968 Kemp choreographed a dance scene for a BBC play The Pistol Shot in the Theatre series, and used Bowie with a dancer, Hermione Farthingale; the pair began dating, and moved into a London flat together. Playing acoustic guitar, Farthingale formed a group with Bowie and bassist John Hitchinson between September

1968 and early 1969 the trio gave a small number of concerts combining folk, Merseybeat, poetry and mime. Bowie and Farthingale broke up in early 1969 when she went to Norway to take part in a film, Song of Norway; this had an impact on him, and several songs, such as "*Letter to Hermione*" and "Life on Mars?" reference her, and for the video accompanying "*Where Are We Now?*" he wore a T-shirt with the words "*Song for Norway*".
They were last together in January 1969 for the filming of Love You till Tuesday, a 30-minute film, not released until 1984, intended as a vehicle to promote him, featuring performances from Bowie's repertoire, including an as yet unreleased "Space Oddity".

After the breakup with Farthingale, Bowie moved in with Mary Finnigan as her lodger. During this period he appeared in a Lyons Maid ice cream commercial, and was rejected for another by Kit Kat. In February and March 1969, he undertook a short tour with Marc Bolan's duo Tyrannosaurus Rex, as third on the bill, performing a mime act. On 11 July 1969, "Space Oddity" was released five days ahead of the Apollo 11 launch, and reached the top five in the UK. Continuing the divergence from rock and roll and blues begun by his work with Farthingale, Bowie joined forces with Finnigan, Christina Ostrom and Barrie Jackson to run a folk club on Sunday nights at the Three Tuns pub in Beckenham High Street.

Influenced by the Arts Lab Movement, this developed into the Beckenham Arts Lab, and became extremely popular. The Arts Lab hosted a free festival in a local park, the subject of his song "Memory of a Free Festival". Bowie's second album followed in November; originally issued in the UK as David Bowie, it caused some confusion with its predecessor of the same name, and the early US release was instead titled Man of Words/Man of Music; it was re-released internationally in 1972 by RCA as Space Oddity. Featuring philosophical post-hippie lyrics on peace, love and morality, its acoustic folk rock occasionally fortified by harder rock, the album was not a commercial success at the time of its release.

Bowie met Angela Barnett in April 1969. They married within a year. Her impact on him was immediate, and her involvement in his career far-reaching, leaving manager Ken Pitt with limited influence which he found frustrating. Having established himself as a solo artist with "Space Oddity", Bowie began to sense a lacking: "a full-time band for gigs and recording—people he could relate to personally". The shortcoming was underlined by his artistic rivalry with Marc Bolan, who was at the time acting as his session guitarist. A band was duly assembled. John Cambridge, a drummer Bowie met at the Arts Lab, was joined by Tony Visconti on bass and Mick Ronson on electric guitar. Known as the Hype, the bandmates created characters for themselves and wore elaborate costumes that prefigured the glam style of the Spiders From Mars. After a disastrous opening gig at the London Roundhouse, they reverted to a configuration presenting Bowie as a solo artist. Their initial studio work was marred by a heated disagreement between Bowie and Cambridge over the latter's drumming style; matters came to a head when Bowie, enraged, accused, "*You're fucking up my album.*" Cambridge summarily quit and was replaced by Mick Woodmansey.

Chapter 2

Iggy Pop looking upwards

The studio sessions continued and resulted in Bowie's third album, The Man Who Sold the World (1970), which contained references to schizophrenia, paranoia, and delusion. Characterized by the heavy rock sound of his new backing band, it was a marked departure from the acoustic guitar and folk rock style established by Space Oddity. To promote it in the US, Mercury Records financed a coast-to-coast publicity tour in which Bowie, between January and February 1971, was interviewed by radio stations and the media. Exploiting his androgynous appearance, the original cover of the UK version unveiled two months later depicted the singer wearing a dress: taking the garment with him, he wore it

during interviews—to the approval of critics, including Rolling Stone's John Mendelsohn who described him as "*ravishing, almost disconcertingly reminiscent of Lauren Bacall*" — and in the street, to mixed reaction including laughter and, in the case of one male pedestrian, producing a gun and telling Bowie to "*kiss my ass*".

During the tour Bowie's observation of two seminal American proto-punk artists led him to develop a concept that eventually found form in the Ziggy Stardust character: a melding of the persona of Iggy Pop with the music of Lou Reed, producing "the ultimate pop idol". A girlfriend recalled his "scrawling notes on a cocktail napkin about a crazy rock star named Iggy or Ziggy", and on his return to England he declared his intention to create a character "who looks like he's landed from Mars".

Hunky Dory (1971) found Visconti, Bowie's producer and bassist, supplanted in both roles by Ken Scott and Trevor Bolder respectively. The album saw the partial return of the fey pop singer of "Space Oddity", with light fare such as "Kooks", a song written for his son, Duncan Zowie Haywood Jones, born on 30 May. Elsewhere, the album explored more serious themes, and found

Bowie paying unusually direct homage to his influences with "Song for Bob Dylan", "Andy Warhol", and "Queen Bitch", a Velvet Underground pastiche. It was not a significant commercial success at the time.

Bowie during the Ziggy Stardust Tour

Dressed in a striking costume, his hair dyed reddish-brown, Bowie launched his Ziggy Stardust stage show with the Spiders from Mars—Ronson, Bolder and Woodmansey—at the Toby Jug pub in Tolworth on 10 February 1972. The show was hugely popular, catapulting him to stardom as he toured the UK over the next six months and creating, as described by Buckley (a music analyst), a *"cult of Bowie"* that was *"unique—its influence lasted longer and has been more creative than perhaps almost any other force within pop fandom."* The Rise and Fall of Ziggy Stardust and the Spiders from Mars (1972), combining the hard rock elements of The Man Who Sold the World with the lighter experimental rock and pop of Hunky Dory, was released in June. "Starman", issued as an April single ahead of the album, was to cement Bowie's UK breakthrough: both single and album charted rapidly following his July Top of the Pops performance of the song. The album, which remained in the chart for two years, was soon joined there by the 6-month-old Hunky Dory. At the same time the non-album single "John, I'm Only Dancing", and "All the Young Dudes", a song he wrote and produced for Mott the Hoople, were successful in the UK. The Ziggy Stardust Tour continued to the United States.

Bowie contributed backing vocals to Lou Reed's 1972 solo breakthrough Transformer, co-producing the album with Mick Ronson. His own Aladdin Sane (1973) topped the UK chart, his first number one album. Described by Bowie as "Ziggy goes to America", it contained songs he wrote while travelling to and across the US during the earlier part of the Ziggy tour.

Bowie's love of acting led his total immersion in the

characters he created for his music. "Offstage I'm a robot. Onstage I achieve emotion. It's probably why I prefer dressing up as Ziggy to being David." With satisfaction came severe personal difficulties: acting the same role over an extended period, it became impossible for him to separate Ziggy Stardust—and, later, the Thin White Duke—from his own character offstage. Ziggy, Bowie said, *"wouldn't leave me alone for years. That was when it all started to go sour ... My whole personality was affected. It became very dangerous. I really did have doubts about my sanity."*

His later Ziggy shows, which included songs from both Ziggy Stardust and Aladdin Sane, were ultra-theatrical affairs filled with shocking stage moments, such as Bowie stripping down to a sumo wrestling loincloth or simulating oral sex with Ronson's guitar. Bowie toured and gave press conferences as Ziggy before a dramatic and abrupt on-stage "retirement" at London's Hammersmith Odeon on 3 July 1973. Footage from the final show was released the same year for the film Ziggy Stardust and the Spiders from Mars.

After breaking up the Spiders from Mars, Bowie attempted to move on from his Ziggy persona. His back catalogue was now highly sought after: The Man Who Sold the World had been re-released in 1972 along with Space Oddity. "Life on Mars?" from Hunky Dory, was released in June 1973 and made number three in the UK singles chart. Entering the same chart in September, Bowie's novelty record from 1967, "The Laughing Gnome", reached number six. Pin Ups, a collection of covers of his 1960s favorites, followed in October, producing a UK number three hit in "Sorrow" and itself peaking at number one, making David Bowie the best-selling act of 1973 in the UK. It brought the total number of Bowie albums concurrently in the UK chart to six.

1974–76: Soul, funk and the Thin White Duke

Bowie moved to the US in 1974, initially staying in New York City before settling in Los Angeles. Diamond Dogs (1974), parts of which found him heading towards soul and funk, was the product of two distinct ideas: a musical based on a wild future in a post-apocalyptic city, and setting George Orwell's 1984 to music. The album went to number one in the UK, spawning the hits "Rebel Rebel" and "Diamond Dogs", and number five in the US. To promote it, Bowie launched the Diamond Dogs Tour, visiting cities in North America between June and December 1974. Choreographed by Toni Basil, and lavishly produced with theatrical special effects, the high-budget stage production was filmed by Alan Yentob. The resulting documentary, Cracked Actor, featured a pasty and emaciated Bowie: the tour coincided with the singer's slide from heavy cocaine use into addiction, producing severe physical debilitation, paranoia and emotional problems. He later commented that the accompanying live album, David Live, ought to have been titled "*David Bowie Is Alive and Well and Living Only in Theory*". David Live nevertheless solidified Bowie's status as a superstar, charting at number two in the UK and number eight in the US. It also spawned a UK number ten hit in Bowie's cover of "*Knock on Wood*". After a break in Philadelphia, where Bowie recorded new material, the tour resumed with a new emphasis on soul.

The fruit of the Philadelphia recording sessions was Young Americans (1975). Biographer Christopher Sandford writes, "Over the years, most British rockers had tried, one way or another, to become black-by-extension. Few had succeeded as Bowie did now. The album's sound, which the singer identified as "plastic soul", constituted a radical shift in style that initially alienated many of his UK devotees. Young Americans yielded Bowie's first US number one, "Fame", co-written with John Lennon, who contributed backing vocals, and Carlos Alomar. Lennon called Bowie's work "*great, but it's just rock'n'roll with lipstick on*".

Earning the distinction of being one of the first white artists to appear on the US variety show Soul Train, Bowie mimed "Fame", as well as "Golden Years". Despite his by now well established superstardom, Bowie, in the words of Sandford, *"for all his record sales (over a million copies of Ziggy Stardust alone), existed essentially on loose change."*

Chapter 3

Bowie's Wild Life and Drug Addiction

The extent to which drug addiction was now affecting Bowie was made public when Russell Harty interviewed the singer for his London Weekend Television talk show in anticipation of the album's supporting tour. Shortly before the satellite-linked interview was scheduled to commence, the death of the Spanish dictator General Franco was announced. Bowie was asked to relinquish the satellite booking, to allow the Spanish Government to put out a live newsfeed. This he refused to do, and his interview went ahead. In the ensuing conversation with Harty, as described by biographer David Buckley, *"the singer made hardly any sense at all throughout what was quite an extensive interview. ... Bowie looked completely disconnected and was hardly able to utter a coherent sentence."*[68] His sanity—by his own later admission—had become twisted from cocaine; he overdosed several times during the year, and was withering physically to an alarming degree. Comments made by Bowie and others in 1976 led to the establishment of Rock Against Racism.

Station to Station's January 1976 release was followed in February by a 3 1/2-month concert tour of Europe and North America. Featuring a starkly lit set, the Isolar – 1976 Tour highlighted songs from the album, including the dramatic and lengthy title track, the ballads "Wild Is the Wind" and "Word on a Wing", and the funkier "TVC 15" and "Stay". The core band that coalesced to produce this album and tour—rhythm guitarist Alomar, bassist George Murray, and drummer Dennis Davis—continued as a stable unit for the remainder of the 1970s. The tour was highly successful but mired in political controversy. Bowie was quoted in Stockholm as saying that *"Britain could benefit from a Fascist leader"*, and was detained by customs on the Russian/Polish border for possessing Nazi paraphernalia.

Matters came to a head in London in May in what became known as the "Victoria Station incident". Arriving in an open-top Mercedes convertible, Bowie waved to the crowd in a gesture that some alleged was a Nazi salute, which was captured on camera and published in NME. Bowie said the photographer simply caught him in mid-wave. He later blamed his pro-Fascism comments and his behavior during the period on his addictions and the character of the Thin White Duke. *"I was out of my mind, totally crazed. The main thing I was functioning on was mythology ... that whole thing about Hitler and Rightism ... I'd discovered King Arthur"*.According to playwright Alan Franks, writing later in The Times, *"he was indeed 'deranged'. He had some very bad experiences with hard drugs."*

1976–79: Berlin era

Bowie moved to Switzerland in 1976, purchasing a chalet in the hills to the north of Lake Geneva. In the new environment, his cocaine use decreased and he found time for other pursuits outside his musical career. He devoted more time to his painting, and produced a number of post-modernist pieces. When on tour, he took to sketching in a notebook, and photographing scenes for later reference. Visiting galleries in Geneva and the Brucke Museum in Berlin, Bowie became, in the words of biographer Christopher Sandford, *"a prolific producer and collector of contemporary art. ... Not only did he become a well-known patron of expressionist art: locked in Clos des Mésanges he began an intensive self-improvement course in classical music and literature, and started work on an autobiography."*

Before the end of 1976, Bowie's interest in the burgeoning German music scene, as well as his drug addiction, prompted him to move to West Berlin to clean up and revitalise his career. While working with Brian Eno and sharing an apartment with Iggy Pop, he began to focus on minimalist, ambient music for the first of three albums, co-produced with Tony Visconti, that became known as his

Berlin Trilogy. During the same period, Iggy Pop, with Bowie as a co-writer and musician, completed his solo album debut The Idiot and its follow-up Lust for Life, touring the UK, Europe, and the US in March and April 1977.

The album Low (1977), partly influenced by the Krautrock sound of Kraftwerk and Neu!, evidenced a move away from narration in Bowie's songwriting to a more abstract musical form in which lyrics were sporadic and optional. Although he completed the album in November 1976, it took his unsettled record company another three months to release it. It received considerable negative criticism upon its release—a release which RCA, anxious to maintain the established commercial momentum, did not welcome, and which Bowie's ex-manager, Tony Defries, who still maintained a significant financial interest in the singer's affairs, tried to prevent. Despite these forebodings, Low yielded the UK number three single "Sound and Vision", and its own performance surpassed that of Station to Station in the UK chart, where it reached number two. Leading contemporary composer Philip Glass described Low as "*a work of genius*" in 1992, when he used it as the basis for his Symphony No.

Chapter 4

Bowie Hit Tracks and Albums

"Heroes" (1977), incorporated pop and rock to a greater extent, seeing Bowie joined by guitarist Robert Fripp. "Heroes" evinced the zeitgeist of the Cold War, symbolised by the divided city of Berlin. Incorporating ambient sounds from a variety of sources including white noise generators, synthesisers and koto, the album was another hit, reaching number three in the UK. Its title track, though only reaching number 24 in the UK singles chart, gained lasting popularity, and within months had been released in both German and French. Towards the end of the year, Bowie performed the song for Marc Bolan's television show Marc, and again two days later for Bing Crosby's final CBS television Christmas special, when he joined Crosby in "Peace on Earth/Little Drummer Boy", a version of "The Little Drummer Boy" with a new, contrapuntal verse. Five years later, the duet proved a worldwide seasonal hit, charting in the UK at number three on Christmas Day, 1982.

After completing Low and "Heroes" album Bowie spent much of 1978 on the Isolar II world tour, bringing the music of the first two Berlin Trilogy albums to almost a million people during 70 concerts in 12 countries. By now he had broken his drug addiction; biographer David Buckley writes that Isolar II was "*Bowie's first tour for five years in which he had probably not anaesthetized himself with copious quantities of cocaine before taking the stage. ... Without the oblivion that drugs had brought, he was now in a healthy enough mental condition to want to make friends.*" The final piece in what Bowie called his "triptych", Lodger (1979), eschewed the minimalist, ambient nature of the other two, making a partial return to the drum- and guitar-based rock and pop of his pre-Berlin era. The result was a complex mixture of new wave and world music, in places incorporating Hijaz non-Western scales.

The album was recorded in Switzerland. Ahead of its release, RCA's Mel Ilberman stated, "*It would be fair to call it Bowie's Sergeant Pepper ... a concept album that portrays the Lodger as a homeless wanderer, shunned and victimized by life's pressures and technology.*" As described by biographer Christopher Sandford, "*The record dashed such high hopes with dubious choices, and production that spelt the end—for fifteen years—of Bowie's partnership with Eno.*" Lodger reached number 4 in the UK and number 20 in the US, and yielded the UK hit singles "Boys Keep Swinging" and "DJ".

Scary Monsters (and Super Creeps) (1980) produced the number one hit "Ashes to Ashes", featuring the textural work of guitar-synthesist Chuck Hammer and revisiting the character of Major Tom from "Space Oddity". The song gave international exposure to the underground New Romantic movement when Bowie visited the London club "Blitz"—the main New Romantic hangout—to recruit several of the regulars (including Steve Strange of the band Visage) to act in the accompanying video, renowned as one of the most innovative of all time. The album's hard rock edge included conspicuous guitar contributions from Robert Fripp, Pete Townshend and Chuck Hammer. As "Ashes to Ashes" hit number one on the UK charts, Bowie opened a three-month run on Broadway on 24 September, starring in The Elephant Man.

Bowie reached a new peak of popularity and commercial success in 1983 with Let's Dance. Co-produced by Chic's Nile Rodgers, the album went platinum in both the UK and the US. Its three singles became top twenty hits in both countries, where its title track reached number one. "Modern Love" and "China Girl" made number two in the UK, accompanied by a pair of acclaimed promotional videos that, as described by biographer David Buckley, "*were totally absorbing and activated key archetypes in the pop world*".

'Let's Dance', with its little narrative surrounding the young Aborigine couple, targeted 'youth', and 'China Girl', with its nude (and later partially censored) beach lovemaking scene (a homage to the film From Here to Eternity), was sufficiently sexually provocative to guarantee heavy rotation on MTV.

By 1983, Bowie had emerged as one of the most important video artists of the day. Let's Dance was followed by the Serious Moonlight Tour, during which Bowie was accompanied by guitarist Earl Slick and backing vocalists Frank and George Simms. The world tour lasted six months and was extremely popular.

Tonight (1984), another dance-oriented album, found Bowie collaborating with Tina Turner and, once again, Iggy Pop. It included a number of cover songs; among them the 1966 Beach Boys hit "God Only Knows". The album bore the transatlantic top ten hit "Blue Jean", itself the inspiration for a short film that won Bowie a Grammy Award for Best Short Form Music Video, "Jazzin' for Blue Jean". Bowie performed at Wembley in 1985 for Live Aid, a multi-venue benefit concert for Ethiopian famine relief. During the event, the video for a fundraising single was premiered, Bowie's duet with Mick Jagger. "Dancing in the Street" quickly went to number one on release.

Bowie was given a role in the 1986 film Absolute Beginners. It was poorly received by critics, but Bowie's theme song rose to number two in the UK charts. He also appeared as Jareth, the Goblin King, in the 1986 Jim Henson film Labyrinth, for which he wrote five songs. His final solo album of the decade was 1987's Never Let Me Down, where he ditched the light sound of his previous two albums, instead offering harder rock with an industrial/techno dance edge.

Chapter 5

Bowie's Achievements

In October 1990, a decade after his divorce with his wife, Bowie and Somali-born supermodel Iman were introduced by a mutual friend. Bowie recalled, "*I was naming the children the night we met ... it was absolutely immediate.*" They married in 1992.

Bowie was inducted into the Rock and Roll Hall of Fame on 17 January 1996. Incorporating experiments in British jungle and drum 'n' bass, Earthling (1997) was a critical and commercial success in the UK and the US, and two singles from the album became UK top 40 hits. Bowie's song "I'm Afraid of Americans" from the Paul Verhoeven film Showgirls was re-recorded for the album, and remixed by Trent Reznor for a single release. The heavy rotation of the accompanying video, also featuring Reznor, contributed to the song's 16-week stay in the US Billboard Hot 100. The Earthling Tour took in Europe and North America between June and November 1997. Bowie reunited with Visconti in 1998 to record "(Safe in This) Sky Life" for The Rugrats Movie. Although the track was edited out of the final cut, it was later re-recorded and released as "Safe" on the B-side of Bowie's 2002 single "Everyone Says 'Hi'". The reunion led to other collaborations including a limited-edition single release version of Placebo's track "Without You I'm Nothing", co-produced by Visconti, with Bowie's harmonized vocal added to the original recording.

Bowie created the soundtrack for Omikron, a 1999 computer game in which he and Iman also appeared as characters. Released the same year and containing re-recorded tracks from Omikron, his album 'Hours...' featured a song with lyrics by the winner of his "Cyber Song Contest" Internet competition, Alex Grant. Making extensive use of live instruments, the album was Bowie's exit from heavy electronica. Sessions for the planned album Toy, intended to feature new versions of some of Bowie's earliest pieces as well as three new songs, commenced in 2000, but the album was never released. Bowie and Visconti continued their collaboration, producing a new album of completely original songs instead in-stead the result of the sessions was the 2002 album Heathen.

In October 2001, Bowie opened the Concert for New York City, a charity event to benefit the victims of the 11 September attacks, with a minimalist performance of Simon & Garfunkel's "America", followed by a full band performance of "Heroes". 2002 saw the release of Heathen, and, during the second half of the year, the Heathen Tour. Taking place in Europe and North America, the tour opened at London's annual Meltdown festival, for which Bowie was that year appointed artistic director. Among the acts he selected for the festival were Philip Glass, Television and the Dandy Warhols. As well as songs from the new album, the tour featured material from Bowie's Low era. Reality (2003) followed, and its accompanying world tour, the A Reality Tour, with an estimated attendance of 722,000, grossed more than any other in 2004. Onstage in Oslo, Norway, on 18 June, Bowie was hit in the eye with a lollipop thrown by a fan; a week later he suffered chest pain while performing at the Hurricane Festival in Scheebel, Germany. Originally thought to be a pinched nerve in his shoulder, the pain was later diagnosed as an acutely blocked coronary artery, requiring an emergency angioplasty in Hamburg. The remaining 14 dates of the tour were cancelled.

In the years following his recuperation from the heart attack, Bowie reduced his musical output, making only one-off appearances on stage and in the studio. He sang in a duet of his 1972 song "Changes" with Butterfly Boucher for the 2004 animated film Shrek

Bowie was awarded the Grammy Lifetime Achievement Award on 8 February 2006. In April, he announced, "I'm taking a year off—no touring, no albums." He made a surprise guest appearance at David Gilmour's 29 May concert at the Royal Albert Hall in London. The event was recorded, and a selection of songs on which he had contributed joint vocals was subsequently released. He performed again in November, alongside Alicia Keys, at the

Black Ball, a New York benefit event for Keep a Child Alive, a performance that marks the last time Bowie performed his music on stage.

Bowie was chosen to curate the 2007 High Line Festival, selecting musicians and artists for the Manhattan event, and performed on Scarlett Johansson's 2008 album of Tom Waits covers, Anywhere I Lay My Head. On the 40th anniversary of the July 1969 moon landing—and Bowie's accompanying commercial breakthrough with "Space Oddity"—EMI released the individual tracks from the original eight-track studio recording of the song, in a 2009 contest inviting members of the public to create a remix. A Reality Tour, a double album of live material from the 2003 concert tour, was released in January 2010.

In late March 2011, Toy, Bowie's previously unreleased album from 2001, was leaked onto the internet, containing material used for Heathen and most of its single B-sides, as well as unheard new versions of his early back catalogue.

Chapter 6

Bowie's Legacy

On 8 January 2013 (his 66th birthday), his website announced a new album, to be titled The Next Day and scheduled for release 8 March for Australia, 12 March for the United States and 11 March for the rest of the world. Bowie's first studio album in a decade, The Next Day contains 14 songs plus 3 bonus tracks. His website acknowledged the length of his hiatus. Record producer Tony Visconti said 29 tracks were recorded for the album, some of which could appear on Bowie's next record, which he might start work on later in 2013. The announcement was accompanied by the immediate release of a single, "Where Are We Now?" written and recorded by Bowie in New York and produced by longtime collaborator Visconti.

A music video for "Where Are We Now?" was released onto Vimeo the same day, directed by New York artist Tony Oursler. The single topped the UK iTunes Chart within hours of its release, and debuted in the UK Singles Chart at No. 6, his first single to enter the top 10 for two decades, (since "Jump They Say" in 1993). A second video, "The Stars (Are Out Tonight)", was released 25 February . On 1 March, the album was made available to stream for free through iTunes. The Next Day debuted at No. 1 on the UK Albums Chart, his first since Black Tie White Noise (1993), and was the fastest-selling album of 2013 at the time. The music video for the song "The Next Day" created some controversy, initially being removed from YouTube for terms-of-service violation, and then restored with a warning recommending viewing only by those 18 or over.

According to The Times, Bowie ruled out ever giving an interview again. An exhibition of Bowie artefacts, called "David Bowie Is", was shown at the Victoria and Albert Museum in 2013. Later that year the exhibition began a world tour, starting in Toronto and including stops in Chicago, Paris, Melbourne, and Groningen (the Netherlands).

Bowie was featured in a cameo vocal in the Arcade Fire song "Reflektor". A poll carried out by BBC History Magazine, in October 2013, named Bowie as the best-dressed Briton in history.

At the 2014 Brit Awards on 19 February, Bowie became the oldest recipient of a Brit Award in the ceremony's history when he won the award for Best British Male, which was collected on his behalf by Kate Moss. His speech read: "*I'm completely delighted to have a Brit for being the best male – but I am, aren't I Kate? Yes. I think it's a great way to end the day. Thank you very, very much and Scotland stay with us.*"

In May 2015, "*Let's Dance*" was announced to be reissued as a yellow vinyl single on 16 July 2015 in conjunction with the "David Bowie is" exhibition at the Australian Centre For The Moving Image in Melbourne.

In August 2015, it was announced that Bowie was writing songs for a Broadway musical based on the SpongeBob SquarePants cartoon series. Bowie wrote and recorded the opening title song to the television series The Last Panthers, which aired in November 2015. The theme that was used for The Last Panthers was also the title track for his January 2016 release Blackstar which is said to take cues from his earlier krautrock influenced work. According to The Times: "*Blackstar may be the oddest work yet from Bowie*".

Bowie's Acting career

Biographer David Buckley writes, "*The essence of Bowie's contribution to popular music can be found in his outstanding ability to analyze and select ideas from outside the mainstream—from art, literature, theatre and film—and to bring them inside, so that the currency of pop is constantly being changed.*" Buckley says, "*Just one person took glam rock to new rarefied heights and invented character-playing in pop, marrying theatre and popular music in one seamless, powerful whole.*"

The beginnings of his acting career predate his commercial breakthrough as a musician. Studying avant-garde theatre and mime under Lindsay Kemp, he was given the role of Cloud in Kemp's 1967 theatrical production Pierrot in Turquoise (later made into the 1970 television film The Looking Glass Murders). In the black-and-white short The Image (1969), he played a ghostly boy who emerges from a troubled artist's painting to haunt him. The same year, the film of Leslie Thomas's 1966 comic novel The Virgin Soldiers saw Bowie make a brief appearance as an extra. In 1976 he earned acclaim for his first major film role, portraying Thomas Jerome Newton, an alien from a dying planet, in The Man Who Fell to Earth, directed by Nicolas Roeg. Just a Gigolo (1979), an Anglo-German co-production directed by David Hemmings, saw Bowie in the lead role as Prussian officer Paul von Przygodski, who, returning from World War I, is discovered by a Baroness (Marlene Dietrich) and put into her Gigolo Stable.

Bowie took the title role in the Broadway theatre production The Elephant Man, which he undertook wearing no stage make-up, and which earned high praise for his expressive performance. He played the part 157 times between 1980 and 1981. Christiane F. – Wir Kinder vom Bahnhof Zoo, a 1981 biographical film focusing on a young girl's drug addiction in West Berlin, featured Bowie in a cameo appearance as himself at a concert in Germany. Its soundtrack album, Christiane F. (1981), featured much material from his Berlin Trilogy albums. Bowie starred in The Hunger (1983), a revisionist vampire film, with Catherine Deneuve and Susan Sarandon. In Nagisa Oshima's film the same year, Merry Christmas, Mr. Lawrence, based on Laurens van der Post's novel The Seed and the Sower, Bowie played Major Jack Celliers, a prisoner of war in a Japanese internment camp. Bowie had a cameo in Yellowbeard, a 1983 pirate comedy created by Monty Python members, and a small part as Colin, the hitman in the 1985 film Into the Night. He declined to play the villain Max Zorin in the James Bond film A View to a Kill (1985).

Absolute Beginners (1986), a rock musical based on Colin MacInnes's 1959 novel about London life, featured Bowie's music and presented him with a minor acting role. The same year, Jim Henson's dark fantasy Labyrinth found him with the part of Jareth, the king of the goblins. Two years later, he played Pontius Pilate in Martin Scorsese's 1988 film The Last Temptation of Christ. Bowie portrayed a disgruntled restaurant employee opposite Rosanna Arquette in The Linguini Incident (1991), and the mysterious FBI agent Phillip Jeffries in David Lynch's Twin Peaks: Fire Walk with Me (1992). He took a small but pivotal role as Andy Warhol in Basquiat, artist/director Julian Schnabel's 1996 biopic of Jean-Michel Basquiat, and co-starred in Giovanni Veronesi's Spaghetti Western Il Mio West (1998, released as Gunslinger's Revenge in the US in 2005) as the most feared gunfighter in the region. He played the ageing gangster Bernie in Andrew Goth's Everybody Loves Sunshine (1999), and appeared in the TV horror serial of The Hunger. In Mr. Rice's Secret (2000), he played the title role as the neighbor of a terminally ill 12-year-old, and the following year appeared as himself in Zoolander.

Bowie portrayed physicist Nikola Tesla in the Christopher Nolan film, The Prestige (2006), which was about the bitter rivalry between two magicians in the late 19th century. In the same year, he voice-acted in the animated film Arthur and the Invisibles as the powerful villain Maltazard and appeared as himself in an episode of the Ricky Gervais television series Extras. In 2007, he lent his voice to the character Lord Royal Highness in the SpongeBob's Atlantis SquarePantis television film. In the 2008 film August, directed by Austin Chick, he played a supporting role as Ogilvie, alongside Josh Hartnett and Rip Torn, with whom he had worked in 1976 for The Man Who Fell to Earth (1976).

Bowie's Music Legacy

From the time of his earliest recordings in the 1960s, Bowie employed a wide variety of musical styles. His early compositions and performances were strongly influenced by rock and rollers like Little Richard and Elvis Presley, and also the wider world of show business. He particularly strove to emulate the British musical theatre singer-songwriter and actor Anthony Newley, whose vocal style he frequently adopted, and made prominent use of for his 1967 debut release. Bowie's music hall fascination continued to surface sporadically alongside such diverse styles as hard rock and heavy metal, soul, psychedelic folk and pop.

Musicologist James Perone observes Bowie's use of octave switches for different repetitions of the same melody, exemplified in his commercial breakthrough single, "Space Oddity", and later in the song "Heroes", to dramatic effect; Perone notes that "*in the lowest part of his vocal register ... his voice has an almost crooner-like richness.*"

Voice instructor Jo Thompson describes Bowie's vocal vibrato technique as "*particularly deliberate and distinctive*". Schinder and Schwartz call him "*a vocalist of extraordinary technical ability, able to pitch his singing to particular effect.*"

Bowie's chamaeleon-like style of music is evident: historiographer Michael Campbell says that Bowie's lyrics "*arrest our ear, without question. But Bowie continually shifts from person to person as he delivers them ... His voice changes dramatically from section to section.*" In a 2014 analysis of 77 "top" artists' vocal ranges, Bowie was 8th, just behind Christina Aguilera and just ahead of Paul McCartney. In addition to the guitar, Bowie was also a fluent player of the keyboard, harmonica, saxophone, stylophone, viola, cello, koto, thumb piano, drums, and percussion.

Bowie's Personal Life

Bowie married Mary Angela Barnett on 19 March 1970 at Bromley Register Office in Bromley, London. They had a son together, Duncan, who was born on 30 May 1971. Bowie and Angela divorced on 8 February 1980 in Switzerland.

On 24 April 1992, Bowie married the Somali-American model Iman in a private ceremony in Lausanne. The wedding was later solemnized on 6 June in Florence. They had one daughter, Alexandria "Lexi" Zahra Jones, born in August 2000. The couple resided primarily in New York City and London, as well as owning an apartment in Sydney.

Bowie declared himself gay in an interview with Michael Watts in the 22 January 1972 issue of Melody Maker, a move which coincided with the first shots in his campaign for stardom as Ziggy Stardust. In a September 1976 interview with Playboy, Bowie said: "*It's true—I am a bisexual. But I can't deny that I've used that fact very well. I suppose it's the best thing that ever happened to me.*"

In a 1983 interview with Rolling Stone, Bowie said his public declaration of bisexuality was "*the biggest mistake I ever made*" and "*I was always a closet heterosexual.*" On other occasions, he said his interest in homosexual and bisexual culture had been more a product of the times and the situation in which he found himself than his own feelings; as described by Buckley, he said he had been driven more by "*a compulsion to flout moral codes than a real biological and psychological state of being.*"

Asked in 2002 whether he still believed his public declaration was the biggest mistake he ever made, he replied "Interesting. [Long pause] I don't think it was a mistake in Europe, but it was a lot tougher in America. I had no problem with people knowing I was bisexual. But I had no inclination to hold any banners nor be a representative of any group of people I knew what I wanted to be, which was a songwriter and a performer, and I felt that bisexuality became my headline over here for so long. America is a very puritanical place, and I think it stood in the way of so much I wanted to do".

It is probably true that Bowie was never gay, nor even consistently actively bisexual ... he did, from time to time, experiment, even if only out of a sense of curiosity and a genuine allegiance with the 'transgressional. Biographer Christopher Sandford says that according to Mary Finnigan, with whom Bowie had an affair in 1969, the singer and his first wife Angie "*lived in a fantasy world ... and they created their bisexual fantasy.*" Sandford tells how, during the marriage, Bowie "*made a positive fetish of repeating the quip that he and his wife had met while 'fucking the same bloke' ... Gay sex was always an anecdotal and laughing matter. That Bowie's actual tastes swung the other way is clear from even a partial tally of his affairs with women.*"

Religion and spirituality

In 2005 he said, "*Questioning my spiritual life has always been germane to what I was writing. Always.*" He added that he was bothered by being "*not quite an atheist*". In the Esquire interview "*What I've Learned*", he stated, "*I'm in awe of the universe, but I don't necessarily believe there's an intelligence or agent behind it. I do have a passion for the visual in religious rituals, though, even though they may be completely empty and bereft of substance. The incense is powerful and provocative, whether Buddhist or Catholic.*" Bowie literally showed an interest in Buddhism that began in 1967. He frequently studied in London under the Tibetan Lama Chime Rinpoche before becoming a solo artist.

Chapter 7

Bowie's Death

On 10 January 2016, two days after his 69th birthday and the release of the album, Blackstar, Bowie died from liver cancer at his New York home. He had been diagnosed with the malignancy eighteen months earlier, but had not made public the news of his illness. Belgian theatre director Ivo van Hove, who worked with the singer on his Off-Broadway musical Lazarus, explained that Bowie was unable to attend rehearsals due to progression of the disease. He noted that Bowie kept working during the illness. Bowie's producer Tony Visconti wrote:

"He always did what he wanted to do. And he wanted to do it his way and he wanted to do it the best way. His death was no different from his life—a work of Art. He made Blackstar for us, his parting gift. I knew for a year this was the way it would be. I wasn't, however, prepared for it. He was an extraordinary man, full of love and life. He will always be with us. For now, it is appropriate to cry."

Legacy and influence

Bowie's innovative songs and stagecraft brought a new dimension to popular music in the early 1970s, strongly influencing both its immediate forms and its subsequent development. A pioneer of glam rock, Bowie, according to music historians Schinder and Schwartz, has joint responsibility with Marc Bolan for creating the genre. At the same time, he inspired the innovators of the punk rock music movement—historian Michael Campbell calls him *"one of punk's seminal influences"*. While punk musicians trashed the conventions of pop stardom, Bowie moved on again—into a more abstract style of music making that in turn became a transforming influence. Biographer David Buckley writes,

"*At a time when punk rock was noisily reclaiming the three-minute pop song in a show of public defiance, Bowie almost completely abandoned traditional rock instrumentation.*" Bowie's record company sought to convey his unique status in popular music with the slogan, "*There is old wave, there is new wave, and there is Bowie.*" Musicologist James Perone credits him with having "*brought sophistication to rock music*", and critical reviews frequently acknowledge the intellectual depth of his work and influence.

Buckley writes that, in an early 1970s pop world that was "*Bloated, self-important, leather-clad, self-satisfied... Bowie challenged the core belief of the rock music of its day.*" According to him "*The one distinguishing feature about early-70s progressive rock was that it didn't progress. Before Bowie came along, people didn't want too much change.*" Further Buckley said "*subverted the whole notion of what it was to be a rock star*", with the result that

"*After Bowie there has been no other pop icon of his stature, because the pop world that produces these rock gods doesn't exist anymore. ... The fierce partisanship of the cult of Bowie was also unique—its influence lasted longer and has been more creative than perhaps almost any other force within pop fandom.*"

Buckley concludes that "*Bowie is both star and icon. The vast body of work he has produced ... has created perhaps the biggest cult in popular culture. ... His influence has been unique in popular culture—he has permeated and altered more lives than any comparable figure.*"

Bowie was inducted into the Rock and Roll Hall of Fame in 1996. Through perpetual reinvention, he has seen his influence continue to broaden and extend: music reviewer Brad Filicky writes that over the decades, "*Bowie has become known as a musical chameleon, changing and dictating trends as much as he has altered his style to fit, influencing fashion and pop culture.*" Biographer Thomas Forget adds, "*Because he has succeeded in so many different styles of music, it is almost impossible to find a popular artist today that has not been influenced by David Bowie.*" In 2000, Bowie was named by NME as the "*most influential artist of all time*".

Bowie was the principal inspiration for the bisexual glam rock icon Brian Slade in the 1998 film Velvet Goldmine.

Awards and recognition

Bowie's 1969 commercial breakthrough, the song "Space Oddity", won him an Ivor Novello Special Award For Originality. For his performance in the 1976 science fiction film The Man Who Fell to Earth, he won a Saturn Award for Best Actor. In the ensuing decades he has been honored with numerous awards for his music and its accompanying videos, receiving, among others, two Grammy Awards and three Brit Awards—winning Best British Male Artist twice and in 1996 the award for Outstanding Contribution to Music.

In 1999, Bowie was made a Commander of the Ordre des Arts et des Letters by the French government. He received an honorary doctorate from Berklee College of Music the same year. He declined the royal honor of Commander of the Order of the British Empire (CBE) in 2000, and turned down a knighthood in 2003. Bowie later stated "*I would never have any intention of accepting anything like that. I seriously don't know what it's for. It's not what I spent my life working for.*"

Throughout his career he sold an estimated 140 million albums. In the United Kingdom, he was awarded 9 Platinum, 11 Gold and 8 Silver albums, and in the United States, 5 Platinum and 7 Gold. In the BBC's 2002 poll of the 100 Greatest Britons, he was ranked 29. In 2004, Rolling Stone magazine ranked him 39th on their list of the 100 Greatest Rock Artists of All Time. Bowie was inducted into the Rock and Roll Hall of Fame on 17 January 1996 and named a member of the Science Fiction and Fantasy Hall of Fame in June 2013.

References

Filicky, Brad (10 June 2002). *"Reviews; David Bowie: Heathen"*. CMJ New Music Report (CMJ) 71 (766): 13.

Mike (2006). *Rock 'n' Roll's Strangest Moments: Extraordinary Tales from Over Fifty Years*. Anova Books. p. 57. ISBN 978-1-86105-923-9. ey (2005): p.19

Thian, Helene Marie (24 March 2015). "Moss Garden". In Eoin Devereux. David Bowie: Critical Perspectives. Routledge. p. 131.
Pegg, Nicholas (2 December 2011). The Complete David Bowie. Titan Books.

Heawood, Sophie (8 January 2013). *"David Bowie has gone from new to old – and what a beautiful thing it is"*. independent.co.uk.

Heatley, Michael; Hopkinson, Frank (24 November 2014). The Girl in the Song: The Real Stories Behind 50 Rock Classics. Anova Books. p. 88. ISBN 978-1-909396-88-3.

Seale, Jack (8 January 2013). *"David Bowie rocks music world with Where Are We Now?"*. radiotimes.com.

Paytress, Mark (5 November 2009). Bolan: The Rise And Fall Of A 20th Century Superstar. Omnibus Press. p. 199. ISBN 978-0-85712-023-6.

McKay, George (1996). Senseless Acts of Beauty: Cultures of Resistance. Verso. p. 188. ISBN 978-1-85984-908-8.

Buckley, Peter, ed. (2003). The Rough Guide to Rock. Rough Guides. p. 130. ISBN 1-84353-105-4.

Roberts, David (ed.) (2001). Guinness World Records: British Hit Singles. Guinness World Records Ltd. p. 120. ISBN 0-85156-156-X.

Bronson, Fred (1990). The Billboard Book of Number 1 Hits. Billboard Books. p. 572. ISBN 0-8230-7677-6.

Timothy, White (May 1983), "David Bowie Interview", Musician magazine (55): 52–66, 122

"(Safe) Sex, (No) Drugs and Rock 'n' Roll : A Star-Filled Send-Off to Freddie Mercury". LA Times. 22 April 1992. Retrieved 11 January 2016.

"David Bowie: Rock and Roll Hall of Fame Induction". rockhall.com. Rock and Roll Hall of Fame. Retrieved 16 September 2010.

"Space Is the Place: Innovative Brooklyn rockers blast off to the future". Spin (Spin Media LLC): 1. June 2006.

Lamb, Charles W.; Hair, Joseph F.; McDaniel, Carl (2007). Marketing. South-Western College Pub. p. 472. ISBN 978-0-324-36208-4.

Stone, Andrew (2008). Denmark. Lonely Planet. p. 46. ISBN 978-1-74104-669-4.

Yuan, Jada (1 May 2006). "*David Bowie Takes Time Off, Sneaks Into Movies*". New York Magazine. Retrieved 16 September 2010.

Gulla, Bob (2008). Guitar Gods: The 25 Players Who Made Rock History. Greenwood. p. 95. ISBN 978-0-313-35806-7.

Gilmore, Mikal (2 February 2012). "How Ziggy Stardust Fell to Earth". Rolling Stone magazine (1149): 36–43, 68.

Marchese, David (May 2008). "The Inquisition: Scarlett Johansson". Spin (Spin Media LLC): 40.

"David Bowie to release "Space Oddity" multi-tracks to celebrate moon landing". NME News. 6 July 2009. Retrieved 2 September 2010.

Diver, Mike (5 February 2010). "*David Bowie A Reality Tour Review*". BBC. Retrieved 2 September 2010.

Perpetua, Matthew (22 March 2011). "*Unreleased David Bowie LP 'Toy' Leaks Online*". Rolling Stone. Retrieved 25 March 2011.
Michaels, Sean (23 March 2011). "*David Bowie's unreleased album Toy leaks online*". The Guardian (UK). Retrieved 25 March 2011.
"*David Bowie To Release New Album and Posts New Music Video*". New York Music News. 8 January 2013. Archived from the original on 30 December 2013. Retrieved 8 January 2013.

"New Website, Album, Single And Video For The Birthday Boy". davidbowie.com. 8 January 2013. Retrieved 8 January 2013.

"David Bowie Returns From Decade-Long Hiatus With New Album, Single". SPIN. Retrieved 22 September 2014.

"David Bowie announces first album in 10 years and releases new single – listen". NME. Retrieved 8 January 2013.

"David Bowie's comeback single rockets to Number One on iTunes". NME. Retrieved 8 January 2013.

"David Bowie secures first Top 10 single in two decades". The Official Chart Company. Retrieved 13 January 2013.

Phillips, Amy (1 March 2013). *"Listen to the New David Bowie Album"*. PitchforkMedia. Retrieved 1 March 2013.

Savage, Lesley (9 May 2013). *"David Bowie's new religious-themed video causing controversy"*. CBS News. Retrieved 10 May 2013.

Teeman, Tim (12 January 2013). "Tony Visconti spills the beans on cocaine, AA and sushi with David Bowie". The Times (London, UK). Archived from the original on 18 January 2013.

"Touring Exhibition: David Bowie is". V&A Museum. Retrieved 24 September 2014.

Barton, Laura. "Arcade Fire: Voodoo rhythms, dance music and David Bowie". The Guardian (London). Retrieved 22 September 2014.

Michaels, Sean. "David Bowie voted the best-dressed person in British history". The Guardian (London). Retrieved 22 September 2014.

"Brit Awards 2014: David Bowie wins best British male award". BBC News. Retrieved 22 September 2014.

"Oldest Brit winner David Bowie enters independence debate". BBC News. 20 February 2014. Retrieved 21 February 2014.

David Bowie on Scottish independence: Reactions on Twitter. The Independent (London, UK). 20 February 2014. Retrieved 21 February 2014.

David Bowie new album: Singer promises new music soon. The Independent (London, UK). Retrieved 22 September 2014.

David Bowie to release retrospective album 'Nothing has Changed' with single 'Sue (Or in a Season of Crime)' in November". Irish Independent (Dublin). Retrieved 22 September 2014.

David Bowie's 'Let's Dance' to get limited vinyl reissue". Never Enough Notes. Never Enough Notes. Retrieved 19 May 2015.

"David Bowie, Aerosmith, Flaming Lips Pen Songs for 'SpongeBob Musical'". Rolling Stone.

"David Bowie to write songs for musical production of SpongeBob SquarePants". Daily Mail. 2 September 2015.

Kreps, Daniel (22 September 2015). "David Bowie Records Theme Song for 'Last Panthers' Series". Rolling Stone. Retrieved 23 September 2015.

Carley, Brennan (24 October 2015). "David Bowie Will Reportedly Release New Album, 'Blackstar,' in January". SPIN. Retrieved 11 January 2016.

Young, Alex (24 October 2015). "David Bowie to release "oddest" album yet, Blackstar, in January". Consequence of Sound. Retrieved 11 January 2016.\

"Zoolander returns: Ben Stiller and Owen Wilson bring blue steel to Paris fashion week". The Guardian. 11 January 2015.

Thompson, Jo (2004). Find Your Voice: A Self-Help Manual for Singers. Artemis Editions. p. 76. ISBN 978-0-634-07435-6.

Kristobak, Ryan (20 May 2014). "Comparing The Top Artists, Past And Present, By Vocal Range". The Huffington Post. Retrieved 22 May 2014.

Pegg, Nicholas (2006). The Complete David Bowie. Reynolds & Hearn. p. 238. ISBN 1-905287-15-1.

.

"*Who knew? Pop superstar David Bowie was once a secret resident of Sydney's Elizabeth Bay*". The Daily Telegraph. 7 May 2014. Retrieved 11 January 2016.\

Watts, Michael (22 January 2006). "On the cusp of fame, Bowie tells Melody Maker he's gay – and changes pop for ever". The Observer. Retrieved 11 August 2012.

"Interview: David Bowie". Playboy. September 1976. Archived from the original on 1 August 2010. Retrieved 14 September 2010.

Andersen, Christopher (July 2012). Mick: the Wild Life and Mad Genius of Jagger. Robson Press. ISBN 978-1-84954-382-8.

"Mick Jagger's affair with David Bowie revealed in new book: They 'were really sexually obsessed with each other'", nydailynews.com; accessed 11 January 2016.

"David Bowie Calls Himself 'A Closet Heterosexual'". orlandosentinel.com (Orlando Sentinel). 30 May 1993. Retrieved 13 May 2012.

Collis, Clark (August 2002). "Dear Superstar: David Bowie". blender.com (Alpha Media Group Inc). Retrieved 16 September 2010.

DeCurtis, Anthony (5 May 2005). In Other Words: Artists Talk About Life And Work. Hal Leonard Corporation. pp. 262–263. ISBN 978-0-634-06655-9. Retrieved 14 May 2012.

"What I've Learned: David Bowie". Esquire. Hearst Communications. 29 February 2004. Retrieved 10 August 2012.

Stardust Memories Without Tibet House, David Bowie never may have gotten Ziggy with it. Now the pop star returns the favor by performing at the annual benefit concert., newsday.com; accessed 11 January 2016.

Adam Perry (February 23, 2011). "Bringing Chogyam Trungpa's "Crazy Wisdom" to the screen — A conversation with filmmaker Johanna Demetrakas". Shambhala Sun. Shambhala SunSpace.

"Flashback: The Clash Rock Against Racism in 1978". Rolling Stone. Retrieved 15 January 2015.

Manzoor, Sarfraz. "1978, the year rock found the power to unite". the Guardian. Retrieved 15 January 2015.

Gilmore, Mikal (18 January 2012). "cover story features David Bowie". Rolling Stone. Retrieved 11 January 2016.

Conlon, James, Ice, Ice, Maybe – Check Out the Hook and Hope Bowie Absolves, retrieved 10 February 2015

Gallagher, Paul (11 January 2016). *"David Bowie died from liver cancer he kept secret from all but handful of people, friend says"*. The Independent.

Sandle, Paul; Faulconbridge, Guy (11 January 2016). *"David Bowie dies after 18-month battle with cancer"*. Reuters. Retrieved 11 January 2016.

"Shock and condolences as the Netherlands reacts to David Bowie's death – DutchNews.nl". DutchNews.nl. 11 January 2016. Retrieved 11 January 2016.

"David Bowie: Friends and stars pay tribute". BBC News. 11 January 2016. Retrieved 11 January 2016.

"David Bowie's Death a 'Work of Art,' Says Tony Visconti". Rolling Stone. Retrieved 11 January 2016.

Campbell, Michael (2011). Popular Music in America:The Beat Goes On. United States: Schirmer. p. 345. ISBN 0840029764.

Paytress, Mark (2003). Bolan: The Rise and Fall of a 20th Century Superstar. Omnibus Press. p. 218. ISBN 978-0-7119-9293-1.

Forget, Thomas (2002). David Bowie (Rock & Roll Hall of Famers). Rosen Publishing Group. p. 7. ISBN 978-0-8239-3523-9.

"Bowie Voted Most Influential Artist by Today's Pop Stars". *NY Rock. 29 November 2000.*

"NME poll places Bowie as most influential artist of all-time". NME. 27 November 2000.

"Grammy Award Winners". Grammy.com. National Academy of Recording Arts & Sciences, Inc. Retrieved 16 September 2010.

"Lifetime Achievement Award: Past Recipients". Grammy.com. National Academy of Recording Arts & Sciences, Inc. Archived from the original on 26 August 2010. Retrieved 16 September 2010.

"Brit Awards 2014: David Bowie wins Best Male and wades into Scottish independence debate via Kate 'Ziggy' Moss". The Independent. 11 January 2015.

Lichfield, John (8 May 2009). "The Big Question: How does the French honours system work, and why has Kylie been decorated?". The Independent (UK). Retrieved 17 September 2010.

Thompson, Jody (8 January 2007). "Sixty things about David Bowie". (No. 35): BBC News. Retrieved 17 September 2010.

(18 April 2015). David Bowie turns down knighthood, music-news.com; retrieved 11 January 2016.

"RIAA Searchable Database: search for David Bowie". Recording Industry Association of America. Retrieved 11 January 2016.

"100 great British heroes". BBC. 11 January 2015.

"100 Greatest Artists: 39 David Bowie". Rolling Stone. 11 January 2015.

"Science Fiction and Fantasy Hall of Fame: EMP welcomes five major players". [June 2013].

"David Bowie: Shape-shifting musician and movie star", empmuseum.org; retrieved 11 September 2013.

"David Bowie spider videos, photos and facts – Heteropoda davidbowie". ARKive. Retrieved 11 January 2016.

Buckley, David (2000) [First published 1999]. Strange Fascination — David Bowie: The Definitive Story. London: Virgin. ISBN 0-7535-0457-X.

Buckley, David (2004). David Bowie: The Complete Guide To His Music. Omnibus Press. ISBN 978-1-84449-423-1.

Buckley, David (2005) [First published 1999]. Strange Fascination — David Bowie: The Definitive Story. London: Virgin. ISBN 978-0-7535-1002-5.

Campbell, Michael (2008). Popular Music in America: And The Beat Goes On. Schirmer. ISBN 978-0-495-50530-3.

Carr, Roy; Murray, Charles Shaar (1981). Bowie: An Illustrated Record. New York: Avon. ISBN 0-380-77966-8.

Cole, Shaun (2000). 'Don we now our gay apparel': gay men's dress in the twentieth century. London: Berg. ISBN 1-85973-415-4.

Ditmore, Melissa Hope (2006). Encyclopedia of Prostitution and Sex Work, Volume 2. Greenwood Publishing Group. ISBN 0-313-32970-2.

Doggett, Peter (2011). The Man Who Sold the World: David Bowie and the 1970s. The Bodley Head. ISBN 978-1-84792-145-1.

Gillman, Peter; Gillman, Leni (1987) [1986]. Alias David Bowie. New English Library. ISBN 0-450-41346-2.

Pegg, Nicholas (2004) [First published 2000]. The Complete David Bowie. London: Reynolds & Hearn. ISBN 1-903111-73-0.

Perone, James E. (2007). The Words and Music of David Bowie. Praeger. ISBN 978-0-275-99245-3.

Sandford, Christopher (1997) [First published 1996]. Bowie: Loving the Alien. Time Warner. ISBN 0-306-80854-4.

Schinder, Scott; Schwartz, Andy (2007). Icons of Rock: An Encyclopedia of the Legends Who Changed Music Forever. Westport, Connecticut: Greenwood Press. ISBN 978-0-313-33845-8.

Thomson, Elizabeth (1993). The Bowie Companion. Macmillan. ISBN 0-283-06262-2.

Thompson, Dave (2006). Hallo Spaceboy: The Rebirth of David Bowie. Ecw Press. ISBN 978-1-55022-733-8.

Cann, David, Any Day Now: David Bowie the London Years 1947–1974, Kenneth Pitt in Books, 2011

Duffy, Chris; Cann, Kevin (2014). Duffy/Bowie Five Sessions (1st UK ed.). ACC Editions. p. 170. ISBN 978-1-85149-765-2.

Greco, Nicholas P., David Bowie in Darkness: A Study of 1. Outside and the Late Career, McFarland & Co., 2015. ISBN 978-0-7864-9410-1

Hendrikse, Wim, Never Get Old. Man of Ch-Ch-Changes Part 1 and Part 2, Gopher Publishers, 2004.

Hendrikse, Wim, David Bowie: The Man Who Changed the World, Authors Online, 2013.

Jacke, Andreas, David Bowie – Station To Station, Psychosozial- Verlag, 2011

Seabrook, Thomas Jerome, Bowie in Berlin: A New Career in a New Town, Jawbone Press, 2008.

Spitz, Marc, Bowie: A Biography, Crown Publishers, 2009.

Trynka, Paul, Starman: David Bowie – The Definitive Biography, Little, Brown Book Group Limited, 2011

Waldrep, Shelton, "*Phenomenology of Performance*", *The Aesthetics of Self-Invention: Oscar Wilde to David Bowie, University of Minnesota Press, 2004.*'

Welch, Chris, David Bowie: We Could Be Heroes: The Stories Behind Every David Bowie Song, Da Capo Press, 1999.